WOMEN

in the

WELL

"It's time women know the truth
about who(se) they are"

LIZ FUERTE

WOMEN in the WELL

"It's time women know the truth about who(se) they are."

Dedication

I dedicate this book to the one who loved me enough to die on a cross HE did not deserve, my Lord and Savior Jesus Christ.

To the most beautiful gift, our Heavenly Father has entrusted me with "Amaris the great" who is a constant reminder of how blessed I am.

To my parents who go out of their way for my baby and I, I love you and thank you for your love and support.

And to you the reader, I pray the Spirit of Truth uses this book as a tool so that you can see, how beautiful and wonderful you truly are, not because of anything you do but because of what was already done.

Table of Contents

Introduction

This book was written for women, from all walks of life who are in desperate need of something more, more than what the world could offer. If you have ever hit "Rock bottom" whether it's spiritual, financial, physical or emotional, then this book is for you!

As a previous Vocational Adult teacher and now a Preacher, I have become skilled at giving practical examples to Spiritual truths and enjoy using modern analogies to make ancient teachings relatable.

I firmly believe that we serve an intentional God that can use anything and anyone to complete His greater purpose. May He use this book as a humble resource to bring you closer to the source.

Jesus answered, "Everyone who drinks this water will be thirsty again, but whoever drinks the water I give them will never thirst. Indeed, the water I give them will become in them a spring of water welling up to eternal life."

John 4:13-14(NIV)

Chapter 1

Step Into The Light

One of my most vivid memories of childhood is being in the car with my family and telling my mother as we drove by one of the biggest hotels I had ever seen, "Someday I will have a hotel like this one and help homeless people have a fresh start". Every morning on our way to school, I would say the same thing and live out the experience in my head believing in my heart somehow, someway, it would come to pass. I knew even then; we were made for so much more than just a "simple" life, I knew I was born for a specific purpose. What I did not know was that one day, I would be that person that needed the "fresh start".

I guess the proper thing to do would be to introduce myself to you and tell you a little bit about who I am or better yet who for a long time, I thought I was.

My story began in Veracruz Mexico with my parents thinking I was a Tumor. I was the "unexpected/unwanted child", the last child my parents would have. When my mother gave birth to me, she said there was a crowd of medical students watching what was a "High risk" delivery. I was not positioned correctly on time, so the doctor had to allow my mother and I to figure it out on our own. In those days, C-Sections were very uncommon unless you had the right kind of money, which meant for us, that was not an option.

It took 48 hours of what my mother calls the worst pain of her life to bring me into the world. The doctor had to allow my infant body to push itself out as my mother did her own pushing, all of this without him moving a finger until I was almost out. At any point in those 48 hours, if my mother's body chose to give out and shut down due to exhaustion, I could have suffocated and not made it out alive. Two days later and exhausted like never before, my mother gave birth to a little baby girl who was also born with two bottom teeth, who she named Elizabeth (Oath of God).

I genuinely think, allowing me to be born breech and with teeth was God's way of letting my parents know that I was going to be a "Natural born rebel". My childhood had so many beautiful moments and not so beautiful moments; It was not uncommon to see people fighting with machetes, snakes under your bed and kids with nothing but underwear on playing in the sand. Our idea of fun was dipping our feet in the swamp and catching whatever little creature was in the water. Those were the good old days.

My parents struggled with alcoholism, and Domestic Violence was a part of everyday life. One day when I was about 5 years old, I remember watching my parents counting money and then finding out they would be leaving us soon for a couple of months with my aunt and begin a new life in the United States. The plan was to save enough money, settle in and then bring us along with them. Before that would happen, I experienced physical child abuse under my aunt's care and suffered greatly without my mother and father.

When my parents had enough money saved, they were able to send for us, and we began a new life here in the beautiful City of Angels. I experienced great culture shock and the mockery of other children due to the language barrier; thank God I learned the language significantly fast. To pay the bills my parents were hardly ever home, and we were left many times with aunts and cousins. Due to the absence of my parents, my elder sister and I became victims of repeated sexual assault by an older cousin, when I finally spoke up, I was immediately silenced by my aunts in fear of my father's retaliation against my cousin.

By the time I hit the teenage years, I was BROKEN! And on a downhill spiral continuously going from bad to worse. At 14 years old I tasted the "Devils cup" for the first time and not only did I like it, but it became my favorite cup, the moment my tongue tasted beer, that was it, I was hooked. That began a momentum of destruction. Partying was involved and living the life I thought would bring some pleasure and take me out of my pain. At 23, I met my Ex-husband and became pregnant with my beautiful little girl.

As excited as I was about becoming a mother, I knew I was with the wrong person. I knew It was my choice and not God's. This would be one of the worse chapters in my life. My ex-husband was an Iraq Veteran and suffered from PTSD; I excused his treatment because I knew he was broken as well and respected what he had done for this Country. Domestic Violence was again part of my "Normal". The strangest thing is that when it comes to him, I can honestly say that the physical aspect of it, was not what left me the deepest scars. The number of times he was unfaithful, and the verbal abuse was what would take years to heal. That part was only healed recently when I finally gave it to God and allowed Him to heal it.

In those years when things were so bad and gradually getting worse, we tried the "Church thing" and even though we attended every Sunday and sometimes weekdays, we maintained the life we had, a life of deliberate sin and wanting to lean only on our own understanding. No change or relief would come from our attempt at a "Christian" life. I mean, I loved the idea of Grace and Jesus being a loving God, but I was in no way ready to walk in love, I also did not feel that too many people resembled what was taught. I watched as my then husband would pray, then come home and be even more abusive as the days went by. Christianity to me was more like a therapy to help me feel better about my life.

I was disillusioned, to say the least and pursuing God for all the wrong reasons. With a selfish heart, I was pretending to seek him while knowing deep inside of me that all I really wanted was to see what I could get out of Him. God was more like a Genie in a lamp whom I could ask anything from, and whether it was good for me or not, He would have to give it to me because I had read somewhere in the Bible, He's both powerful and loving. I wanted a full-time God on a Part-time relationship, that's if you can call an hour on Sundays, a "relationship". It was mostly a one-way street where God had to do it my way or the highway, in our relationship I was the "Abuser".

On top of all of that, I had the most judgmental heart known to men, and in the misunderstanding of Grace, I believed we still had to earn our way to heaven by having to be perfect. I had no true revelation of His Grace at all, I mean, how could I? If I didn't want to get to know the giver of that Grace. I was expecting people to be what I now realized is impossible! They were all in my mind supposed to be mini-Jesus who were to not ever think of, intent to or act on sin and if for one second they were weak and slipped, then that would make them "Hypocrites" when what really makes people "Hypocrites" is pretending that they have no sin, and acting as if they alone have their lives under control. It is only now that I understand the meaning of Grace, His undeserving favor towards ALL His children.

There was no humility in me; there was no surrender, no letting go and letting God. Without knowing it, I was playing God and judging others without looking at myself. I was looking at God's children through the eyes of Satan himself who is referred to in the bible as "the accuser". For so many years I pretended to believe in our Heavenly Father, when all I did, was doubt Him. With true believe comes obedience and at that time in my life, obedience was not going to work for me.

When my ex-husband and I threw in the towel, I placed all the blame on God, I think my prayers went something like this "God, I prayed, and I prayed, and in the Bible it says that you would do all of these amazing things and you didn't, you must not be real, what kind of God allows divorce when He says in the Bible He loves marriages"?! I didn't just divorce my ex, in that moment, I filed for divorce from God. I say filed because even though I wanted to leave Him, He never left me. He did, however, allow me the freedom to make my own choices and the more I attempted to separate myself from Him the wider I cracked open the door that allowed the enemy of my soul to have his shot at taking me out and to be very honest, he almost did.

A new quest for spirituality was on the horizon and the more knowledgeable I became in this "New Age" movement that is so popular today, the more ridiculous Christianity sounded. I truly believed with all my heart that anyone who bought the "Superman" of the Middle East story must also believe in dragons and unicorns. The enemy is so good at what he does that the darker I became, the more spiritually enlightened I believed I was.

I actually thought I was far above the ignorant crowd when in fact I was the most ignorant of them all. I was in no way enlightened, the further away I was from the only way, the only truth and the only life who is our Lord and Savior Jesus Christ, the further into the dark abyss I fell.

I was so passionate about this quest for all these different ways to God or Goddess for that matter that I began to use my true God-given talents as counterfeit. I agreed to accompany an African Shaman to his "Spiritual Hospital" in Hollywood where we would practice different types of energy healing rituals on people who were as confused as I was and in the same level of desperation, seeking some type of hope. I even welcomed a lady to my apartment on the weekdays who would teach us Transcendental Meditation. According to her, what she taught by a "Master Teacher" in India was one of the most powerful ways to reach the God within.

The enemy knew of the prophetic gift God put in me and made sure I was enticed enough in my vulnerable state to use it all onto him. So much so, that I even got certified as a Hypnotherapist and became skilled at reading the tarot. I sure was living the "vibrate at a higher frequency, do what pleases you, have fun in this life because if you get it wrong you will only come back recycled somehow in the reincarnation process, and we are all Gods" type of lifestyle. I thought I was as enlightened as you can spiritually get when I was in fact, as confused as they come.

None of this vibration thing was working. There was only so many Crystals I could buy, incense I could burn and classes I could take. I was hurting; I was hurting BAD! By the time I turned thirty-two, I had already experienced every type of Abuse you can think of, literally every type! I had also gone through a divorce, homelessness, a seven year on and off custody battle and a betrayal that came from those closest to me. My future looked bright and promising, and in case you didn't catch the sarcasm, by that I mean, I was suicidal! I had become a full-blown alcoholic who was unstable, at my heaviest weight ever, single and so not ready to mingle due to the rage inside of me from the aftermath of the distress.

That's when the true "I AM" called me from darkness into light. The just another "Master Teacher" as I referred to Him in my ignorance made Himself known to me so lovingly in a time of utter despair. I once heard a preacher say, "Sometimes you have to hit rock bottom to find out who the rock is at the bottom". Well, let me tell you, for me no other statement was a better fit.

The events that led to this life-changing experience included a friend who would constantly pray for me and speak to me about Jesus even when I would beg him to stop. I now understand why he entered my life at just the right time and I don't believe it's any coincidence that his name is Emmanuel which means "God is with us" in Hebrew.

Emmanuel became a prayer warrior who partnered up with God to bring His black sheep back. He would always talk about the love of the King of Kings and cry due to the passion he felt deep within his soul. I could sense that there was power in his words and as much as I would so eloquently tell him to "put a sock in it", I must be honest, he sparked curiosity in me. I was such an ugly person to him, yet, he would never cease to pray, and even when I would pass out drunk he would pray, pray, pray!

His original hometown is Las Vegas Nevada and it was time for him to leave California when he said "I want to take you somewhere one last time before I leave" when we arrived, I looked at our special tree where we had sat many times before and starred into the ocean together as he began to....yup you guessed it.... pray. I was consumed with sadness because of his departure, and all I can clearly remember is those fateful words "Father God, please use my friend and don't ever give up on her". As we went back towards the car everything felt the same, nothing looked any different, but little did I know something had happened in the Spiritual realm that would forever change the course of my life.

Some weeks had passed when one night as I was sobering up, I heard a very soft whisper say "step into the light" I said those words out loud in a questioning tone and started looking around to find the source. When I didn't find any possibilities, I went ahead and blamed the state I was in and decided just to let it go. Approximately two nights after that incident, Jesus himself came to me in a dream and while holding my friend Emmanuel as if they were best friends said to me "I used him to bring you back". I have always been the type to have dreams, and usually, they don't amaze me, but this dream was different, this dream had power, this dream I KNOW was straight from GOD!

When I woke up, still in shock and awe of the feelings involved with this very vivid dream, I could not help but to get on my knees and apologize for all my previous blasphemy, I said "Lord I know this is you, Jesus, I know you are the son of God, and I don't know how but I want to follow you! I want to serve you; I want to know you, the real you."

For the first time in my life, the Prince of Peace became far more than a picture or a statue in a building. He was no longer a "Master Teacher" in the same category in my faith chart as the tooth fairy, Santa Claus or even the elf on the shelf. I knew the Almighty Himself called me by name and in the perfect time, right when I was on the verge of spiritual death. He knew I was ready to throw in the towel and being the amazing Redeemer that He is; He saved me.

As much as I wish I could tell you I was sanctified right after that, the truth is, I was nowhere near it. To this day which is almost 3 years ago, God has and will continue to transform me through this beautifully painful process called LIFE. I have learned, however, in this walk with

Christ that one of the reasons we can't skip the "Earth" experience has to do with that sanctification process and our purpose in it. I have learned that the more we surrender in mind, body, and Spirit, the more He can work in us and through us. I have become clear of the fact that the "Promise land" can take us 11 days or 40 years and that part is mostly, up to us.

Today, I am happy to say I have been delivered from alcoholism, became Co-Pastor at a Motel Ministry through Saddleback, and Founded Liz Fuerte Ministries. Most importantly, for the first time in my life, I have a close relationship with the Creator of it All.

So why the book? Why write "Women in the Well"?

One morning as I began my day with praise music, I heard "Women in the Well" in my Spirit. Being the humble person that I am, I corrected God and said, "Lord it's woman at the well" God replied, "I want you to teach women to live IN ME", and the rest is history. I believe this book is not just written by me but through me. I also believe that whoever reads it and is ready to follow everything in it will see breakthrough like never before. This is not just a book that will be a treat to the reader, this book I believe and declare has an anointing to change LIVES!

With that being said, it is crucial that we have a revelation of the importance of our participation in the Savior's plan. Can a tree grow without planting a seed? We too must plant seeds that only He can grow.

God does not play favorites, and what He has done for me in this past couple of years He can also do for you and even greater, even faster! God is not restricted by time, the more you learn to surrender to Him, walk in obedience and deal with what He reveals for you to heal, the faster you will mature and the more He will manifest His resurrection power in your life. We serve a mighty God that truly wants to go above and beyond what we can ask or think through us, but here is the Catch...He will not do it FOR us, it must be done THROUGH us. That means we must choose to Take Action.

Are you girls ready?

Let's step into the light.

But you are not like that, for you are a chosen people. You are royal priest, a holy nation, God's very own possession. As a result, you can show others the goodness of God, for he called you out of the darkness into his wonderful light.

1Peter2:9(NLT)

Chapter 2

Your choices are not your identity

One Halloween night I remember sewing costumes for my family which consisted of my husband at the time, my 4-year-old daughter and myself. I was so excited about dressing up as Smurfette that even though that gooey stuff almost peeled off my face, the experience seemed well worth it. That night we captivated so many people's attention, and I must say, I felt pretty proud. There we were parading proudly, two Smurfettes and Papa Smurf, it was the cutesiest site ever.

Before the night ended, my ex-husband made sure he accomplished his goal of putting me down enough to ruin my night. As it was his habit, he added some extra colorful names to our costumes, naming my daughter baby Smurf, keeping his as Papa Smurf and naming me Ugly Smurf. I remember thinking I looked great throughout the night, which is until he reminded me of my "Reality". It only took that single moment to corrupt my perception into his and all I saw after that was Ugly Smurf.

I constantly heard things like, "you disgust me, what are you even good for, and I'm not in love with you, and if I find someone else, I will cheat on you". As a Latina woman coming from a family background where divorce was not an option, I figured, this was it, this would be my life, I was officially, STUCK! I had received so many lies into my Spirit, that for many years I questioned my existence since the man I was in love with, thought all of these heartbreaking things about me. I would experience bouts of depression and stay in bed immobile for days at a time, finding relief only by imagining how, I could just end it all, least painfully.

When I managed to get up out of bed, it would only be to drink my sorrows away and survive just one more day. I was not living; I was only existing. My reality was tainted by the nightmare that kept me blind about who I truly was. I saw myself through the prism of his hate, not through the eyes of God's love.

I can't help but wonder who you have chosen to believe? As I write this book, I also wonder what behaviors you adopted as your own to validate what is said about who you are. Did you maybe become meaner, more selfish, and irresponsible or a procrastinator because that's what people said you were and their opinions of you mattered so much, that they have now become your reality? Or do you believe you are weak and worthless incapable of truly ever being loved and unaware of the calling in your life? If this is where you stand, then let me tell you the Truth about the only perception that matters, the perception of the Living God.

You are a DAUGHTER of the KING! A true work of Art, who He loves with an everlasting Love. So much love that He sent his only son to die for you, now I don't know about you, but I don't care how much I love a person, I am not giving up my daughter for anybody.

Yet, the creator of the Universe, the one who made all the galaxies, the sun, moon and everything under it, is the same God that sent his son to die for YOU! To simply hear the truth once, twice or even a thousand times, won't do much, but if you ask God to give you a Spiritual revelation of this truth, only then can it become a part of your reality and when that happens, you will begin to walk in the fullness of who you really are.

Through pain and heartbreak, it can become too foggy for any of us to see, and the enemy of our soul doesn't care how much we attend church or pretend to others that we are happy, as long as we don't know our identity. The enemy knows that in this state we are harmless to the kingdom of darkness. Not only that, but we will do Satan's job for him! Just like I was killing myself at the bar, you too will use your God-given AUTHORITY against yourself; it's like cheering for the wrong team when you are unfamiliar with the game. When we are not aware of the devil's schemes, we will mistakenly help him destroy every promise in our lives and not even have a clue we are doing it.

If you are in the dark about your TRUE IDENTITY, you will forfeit any power given to you as a birthright which carries the anointing to become His co-participants in the saving of other people's souls. The power that I'm talking about could never be earned, but it is freely given to you by His undeserved Grace.

It is important that we understand that Satan has a hidden agenda and has been working on you from the moment you were born and even before then, through your family. There is something called Generational curses, and because this topic is worthy of its own book, I would not dare to explain it here. I do however, encourage you to do your research on this matter so you can begin to understand why certain things can run through the family and are extremely difficult if not impossible on our own strength to break. To every "bad news" there will always be "good news", GOD can break these!!

For things to shift in the physical, they must first shift in the Spiritual, and that's where our Father comes in. When we allow His Light to reveal all of these sins and weaknesses that we have been dealing with so secretly, He can then heal them and break them once and for all, the chains that have kept us in bondage for so many years. From that point, we can exercise our ability to choose, and instead of swimming against the current, we can begin to flow with the tide.

Have you ever heard this "You are such a witch (spelled a bit differently), lazy, overbearing, annoying, dumb, and we could go on and on with all of these creative words we have collected throughout generations...Well, here's the truth, YOU are not!! You may at one point or another have chosen to be all of these things and hopefully not at the same time, but this comes down to it being that, not WHO you are but who you chose to be.

Ready for a cool story? There was a man named Simon, back in the "Bible days" names were far more descriptive, in those days, they were more like "labels". Can you believe people labeled you right of the bat? Brutal!

Simon meant "The listener" when Jesus met Simon that's what Simon believed he was just a simple "Listener", so that's who he chose to be. However, when Jesus called Simon to serve him, he told him the TRUTH of who he was. He changed his name to Peter which meant "Rock" and not only did Jesus change his name, but he prophesied over him that he would be the rock on which Jesus would build his church, and that is exactly what he did. If Simon would have said "Jesus, I can't preach the gospel! My name is not Speaker, I was born to just listen" Simon Peter would have relinquished the calling in his life, but because he decided to become not what he was told he was born to be, but who Jesus said he was, he went on to be one of the most important figures in the Bible who spoke the word of God boldly.

There is a TRUTH to everyone that does not agree with all the lies you have been told. Maybe you also have been called a Simon, when you are really a PETER. We tend to accept the labels people have placed on us and reinforce them by making choices that reflect those labels.

There is another aspect that influences our distorted perception of who we really are. This one we will call the "Monkey see Monkey do" component. This is a lot more common, and I'm sure you are familiar with it. Let's use another example to help us see this objectively. If you saw a little boy next to his dad pretending he was drinking a beer and dancing, I bet you would laugh because let's face it; anything kids do is cute. I just recently saw a video of a child approximately 3 years old, and he was dancing holding what looked like, an alcoholic beverage and looking ready to draw his gun.... At 3 years old!!!! I can't lie to you, I thought he looked adorable, but I soon became sad at the thought of what this little boy could later become.

I want to give you another example, and this time our "Subject" is a little girl. Let's say this little girl is naturally bubbly, fierce, loves to dance and speaks her mind but because her mother grew up in a "Children are to be seen and not heard" manner she instructs her daughter never to ask questions, not be so "all over the place" and stop dancing so much. What do you think would become of this little girl? I personally believe she would think there was something terribly wrong with her and the spark that made her so bright would soon lose its luster.

Then you have the awesome teenage years where her body begins to change and experiences all of these hormones which make her body feel like the enemy number one and begins to hear "You are moody, you're weird, you're such a witch (again spelled a little different) what then do you think she will continue to become. As if all of this was not enough to break a girl down, she has society telling her she's too fat, skinny, tall, short, ugly, fake and so on and so forth. Lastly, she has the whispers of the enemy in her head, which she thinks are her own thoughts, but we know, are not. The enemy has power in an unseen realm that we have disregarded in the belief that it is fantasy, but I can attest to that fact that it's not; here is some scripture to prove it.

You used to live in sin, just like the rest of the world, obeying the devil--the commander of the powers in the unseen world. He is the spirit at work in the hearts of those who refuse to obey God.

Ephesians 2:2(NLT)

After all of this, do you still think this beautiful vibrant little girl can live a good life without God?

No, she can't, and neither can we. Life is a fight, and when we team up with our daddy in heaven, we have a shot at fighting the good fight and stopping the influence of the enemy in our lives. Here's even more good news, we have access to the right kind of armor here on this earthly realm, to become more than conquerors. We can overcome it all when we partner up with God, only then can we be sure to WIN!

Finally, be strong in the LORD and in his mighty power. Put on the full armor of God, so that you can

take your stand against the devil's schemes. For our struggle is not against flesh and blood, but against the rulers, against the authorities, against the powers of this dark world and against the spiritual forces of evil in the heavenly realms. Therefore put on the full armor of God, so that when the day of evil comes, you may be able to stand your ground, and after you have done everything, to stand. Stand firm then, with the belt of truth buckled around your waist, with the breastplate of righteousness in place, and with your feet fitted with the readiness that comes from the gospel of peace. In addition to all this, take up the shield of faith, with which you can extinguish all the flaming arrows of the evil one. Take the helmet of salvation and the sword of the Spirit, which is the word of God.

Ephesians 6:10-18(NIV)

For too many years I hated myself, I believed all the lies that had been fed into my spirit and was ignorant of the truth. I was not able to function without alcohol, and I became my own worst nightmare. After years of what felt like near death hangovers, I was done, but as much as I tried to drop alcohol on my own, I simply could not. I remember one specific day I was drinking in the park and after 18 years of drinking, I just could not take the guilt and shame anymore.

I had prayed many times before, but this time felt different. I was ready to make my move and finally invite Him into a partnership with me, so I said, "Ok God if you really can take this from me then do it, do it NOW, show me your Glory! I will do my part and choose to believe I am free but it's you who has to take this addiction from me."

As it is very common in my life I experienced a dream where I saw a demon with a Lizard looking body screaming and crying out tears of blood, and when I woke up I knew in my Spirit; I was delivered from alcoholism, just like that in a moment He broke off those chains. I had gone to AA meetings many times before and to be honest, I would "hit the bar" as soon as I would leave. Alcohol was mentioned so much that instead of not wanting it, I craved it even more. To me it was like loving tacos and talking about tacos for an hour, now let's be clear about something, I am in no way saying AA does not work because for so many out there it absolutely has, what I am saying is, it did not work for me.

Not a DUI with all its mandatory programs, not a New Year's resolution, not even seeing my daughter cry because she hated the very sight of me with a drink in hand, Nothing!! Only God did what I could not do, and when He delivered me, He took my choice and made it part of my reality.

I became a Sober woman with no cravings or desire to drink, and even when my peers tempted me, the choice between God's promise in my life and the bottle was crystal clear. He is so FAITHFUL! He truly did show me His Glory.

I believe that He wants this for you as well and He can if you let Him. All you have to do is ASK and then CHOOSE.

If you are anything like I was then you are probably thinking "nope not me, I can't shake this addiction off. I've tried, and I've tried only to relapse again and again" well good, you are a perfect candidate for this experiment, try this formula and partner up with God. Knowing that on your own, you are not able is a perfect place to be, in this way you will give him all the credit and see the true power of his Glory! Be patient and trust him, he can do it, but only through you.

Now to him who is able to do immeasurably more than all we ask or imagine, according to his power that is at work within us,

Ephesians3:20(NIV)

The more I walk with Christ and the further I walk away from my old life, the more I realize that the reason why we are feeling so "stuck" is that we truly believe we are alone and we are not. We have a God that is ready to help us when we call on Him and want to work through us but needs our full participation. Notice the verse above states; He is willing to do immeasurably more than what we can ask or even imagine within us which means through us, doesn't say, for us, it says through us. This means most of us are waiting on God when He has been waiting for us.

Who are you? Let me rephrase that question, who do you think you are?

What names or titles did you accept as your reality and do you want to keep them or choose better?

Do you want a better life?

If you have never dealt with any issues of addiction, then consider yourself blessed. Some people live perfectly "normal lives," but normal doesn't mean fulfilled. In my experience as a life coach, I have found that a lot of women who do not "rock the boat" for fear of rejection, have lost a sense of who they are and not using your natural gifts can also be a recipe for internal disaster.

If this strikes a chord, then here is my advice, know your "Foundation first". Here is one of my favorite examples to use when trying to explain to women, who have felt they were stagnant and struggled with feelings of "being lost". Imagine a fish and a bird decide to compete; the first competition is a swimming one, who do you think will win? How about a flying competition, who do you think will win that one? Now if a bird loses at a swimming competition does this make the bird a loser? NO, it means this bird was born to fly.

I have found that most women go around life not knowing their strengths or God-given talents. They go around stressing wanting to be the best "swimmers" when they were born to fly. Yes, you were born with natural abilities, natural talents and it's time to unleash them and let God use them for His Glory. Here is a parable Jesus used to portray what I just stated.

For the kingdom of heaven is as a man traveling into a far country, who called his own servants, and delivered unto them his goods.

And unto one he gave five talents, to another two, and to another one; to every man according to his several ability; and straightway took his journey. Then he that had received the five talents went and traded with the same and made them other five talents.

And likewise, he that had received two, he also gained other two.

But he that had received one went and digged in the earth and hid his lord's money.

After a long time the lord of those servants cometh, and reckoneth with them.

And so he that had received five talents came and brought other five talents, saying, Lord, thou deliveredst unto me five talents: behold, I have gained beside them five talents more. His lord said unto him, Well done, thou good and faithful servant: thou hast been faithful over a few things, I will make thee ruler over many things: enter thou into the joy of thy lord.

He also that had received two talents came and said, Lord, thou deliveredst unto me two talents: behold, I have gained two other talents beside them. His lord said unto him, Well done, good and faithful servant; thou hast been faithful over a few things, I will make thee ruler over many things: enter thou into the joy of thy lord.

Then he which had received the one talent came and said, lord, I knew thee that thou art an hard man, reaping where thou hast not sown, and gathering where thou hast not strawed:

And I was afraid and went and hid thy talent in the earth: lo, there thou hast that is thine. His lord answered and said unto him, Thou wicked and slothful servant, thou knewest that I reap where I sowed not, and gather where I have not strawed: Thou oughtest therefore to have put my money to the exchangers, and then at my coming I should have received mine own with usury. Take therefore the talent from him, and give it unto him which hath ten talents.

For unto every one that hath shall be given, and he shall have abundance: but from him that hath not shall be taken away even that which he hath.

Matthew 25:14-29(KJV)

Now I don't know about you, but I don't want to be that servant that hid his talent, and it was taken away from him. I want to be that servant who used all of his

God-given talents and because of that God gave him even more. I want with all of my heart to see my Creator someday and hear those words "Well done, good and faithful servant".

How about you?

What can you do today to get one step closer to becoming all God created you to be?

When you decide to come into agreement with who God says you are and move forward in the knowledge that you have of yourself and most importantly God, you will begin to walk, then run towards your destiny. A destiny that has always been available to you from the start.

If a part of you feels scared, know that this is absolutely normal, I think I would be more concerned if you had no feelings at all. We all crawl into or out of things at first as we begin any journey and maybe this exercise will help.

Earlier this week my daughter and I were having a conversation about her session with her counselor. She is 11 now and has had a counselor since she was five, due to the entire crisis we have faced together. After 6 years of therapy both her counselor and I have agreed that it's time for her to put into practice everything she learned and face life without her. Next week will be her last session, so her counselor is winging her off the sessions and equipping her to be her own support in times where she was able to rely on the weekly appointments.

She taught her a "Jar exercise," and when Amaris shared it with me immediately I said, "This is going in the book". It's very simple yet powerful, she gave Amaris a little Jar and in it had Amaris write herself different love notes/words of encouragement, every time Amaris takes one out to read it she is to put another one in the jar and dispose of the last one. This keeps it fresh, so the words don't become ineffective due to repetition and to activate the long-term memory in her brain caused by writing.

How Genius! Something so simple that we can all learn from because let's face it, we ALL need it. Drown out all of the enemies lies and become co-participant with God! Success will be inevitable. We will walk in the truth of who we were made to be, MORE THAN CONQUERORS!!

"7 easy yet POWERFUL questions that are sure to give you clarity about your purpose"

Worksheet

https://www.lizfuerteministries.com/p/
free-gift-7-easy-yet-POWERFUL

Chapter 3

His way, His will, His time

In the Summer of 2016, my daughter and I went into the Salvation Army to live for about 4 months. I have always struggled with having a "Big mouth" and can't seem to be quiet when something feels unjust. The ladies there started realizing that I was not the one to stay quiet and to put it gently, I was not very well-liked. There was a self-proclaimed "Bully" living with us who managed to terrorize most of the girls and mistreat her own son. I, of course, would not stand for it and made sure she knew of my disapproval of her actions. After about four months, I had it with her! I had become an employee of the department of children and family services, and she was not happy about that. She had lost custody of two children and hated everything the department stood for.

When she found out I got hired by that department, it was as if I took her kids myself and her behavior towards me took a turn for the worse. One morning when everyone was getting in line to get their breakfast, "prison style" she made a scene and started telling everyone out loud to hide their kids from me because I would take them. I was so tired of her tyranny, and by the way, I was not so "spiritually mature" then, so I decided to approach her table and said, "Is there something, you need to tell me"? In a very classy manner, she responded, "yea let's go outside", to let her know I meant business I said, "Let's go, I'm not afraid of you" We got into a confrontation, and it got so bad that everyone under the same roof had to get involved.

We both got escorted to our rooms, and I remember getting on my knees to pray, first to repent and then to ask for help. I prayed what I believe to be one of the most powerful psalms in the Bible, Psalm 91:1 I call it my 911 prayer. I heard a knock at the door and when I saw the face of our social worker I knew it was bad. We both individually got called in, and we both individually got kicked out. I was mad! I put all the blame for my inability to control my anger and later focused it on God. In that psalm, it mentions that we will see the punishment of the wicked and when we both got kicked out, something just did not add up. I was not on speaking terms with God, I stopped praying, and when I could get myself to talk to Him, it was just to tell him how disappointed in Him I was. Like a rebellious teenage kid throwing a tantrum, I wanted everything my way, and despite my actions for that moment I thought I knew more than God.

I was able to get over it after some time and became even closer to God than I initially was. Six months later during a 21day fast, I was praying in my car and reading my bible when I heard a voice say, "So this is where you work"? I looked to my left, and there she was my nemesis, or so I thought. She asked me "Are you reading the bible"? I told her I was; she began to sob uncontrollably while trying to tell me in between tears she had lost her 3rd son to the system and was living on the streets. From the day she left the Salvation Army according to her, things went from bad to worse.

I could not help but to feel compassion and asked for permission to pray for her, as I laid hands on her, I could feel the power of God and his undeserving Grace. When I got home that same day, I remember going into my bible study app and the study for that evening was Psalm 91:1!!!

My eyes kept gazing at the part that said, "You will only observe with your eyes and see the punishment of the wicked". I was sad that she had experienced such despair; I was also in AWE of the faithful God we serve who keeps His word, no matter how long it takes. I gave her my number, and we kept in contact, we would even ride to church together, and I watched as she was watered, baptized and gave her life to the Lord.

We serve a God who is not bipolar, doesn't have dementia and is not in any way a liar. Sometimes, things take a little longer than we wish they would and other times we won't get what we want at all but if we trust God, maintain a hopeful heart along with a grateful attitude, what the waiting period will do in your character will be far better for your life than any end result.

Not only so, but we also glory in our sufferings, because we know that suffering produces perseverance; perseverance, character; and character, hope.

Romans 5:3-4(NIV)

like any good father, He wants what is best for us and even though sometimes our comfort is at stake. He knows that our character is worth the wait. He does not do this because it pleases Him to see us miserable, as a matter of fact, it is quite the contrary. God really wants to bless us with the desires of our heart, but He wants to make sure we are ready to receive them.

Do you know what desire means? The word De-sire comes from Latin meaning "of the Father". Any deep desire in your heart that agrees with His word, He put there! In your heart! Why would He not want what He put in you to accomplish from the start?

Take delight in the LORD, and he will give you the desires of your heart.

Psalm 37:4(NIV)

When we are not aware of this, we believe that what we desire is somehow impossible to get. We think that some gifts He endowed us with, are not gifts but curses.

Remember my struggle with my "big mouth"? For many years, I was very hard on myself; I wondered why I couldn't just be quiet! I was like the local volunteer hero every time I would see any type of injustice, even though everyone in the room would keep silent, I simply could not. I wasn't just passionate about injustice I was also plain loud; you know those obnoxious people in groups that talk and talk, well..... guilty as charged.

I could tell people were annoyed and uncomfortable because I was not afraid to speak the truth, and this kept me lonely and ashamed. I had a lack of self-control, and my inability to be "normal" was torturous due to the ignorance of these gifts. I was not allowing God to mature them in me and they created more strife than peace, I could not stand myself. I remember leaving church groups or even gatherings with friends and really feeling bad about who I was. I wished for so long to have the ability to just "zip my lip".

"Before I formed you in the womb I knew you, before you were born I set you apart; I appointed you as a prophet to the nations."

Jeremiah 1:5(NIV)

For something to be formed, it requires many pieces and when I gave my life to Christ that verse kept showing up. I felt it was an invitation to pursue a journey and find out what He put in me that I was not aware of. I was intrigued by the fact that I thought my life started when I was born, and the Bible said it started way before then, as humans trying to understand an eternal God, that is almost too deep to comprehend, but because I decided to say yes to God, I was willing to give it a shot.

I went ahead and took many different personality test and communicator, teacher; preacher kept showing up on all my results, that's when I realized "No wonder I can't be quiet"! I was not born to be quiet! I was born to be a preacher of the word of God. He can use my "Big mouth" for his will; I also have gifts of Faith, exhortation(motivation) and many more that allowed me to see why I struggled so much. I was not positively using my talents! I thought they were a curse when in fact they were a blessing. I began to gain wisdom through reading and hearing the word of God, and now I am using every gift I have unto the purpose for which it was made.

One of the most interesting things to me about this journey is that it began with me wanting to know more about God and in the process, I have learned more about me than I ever knew before. Now, instead of numbing my gifts with alcohol, I use them for His Glory. I would be lying if I told you my life is perfect because it's far from that. We are here on earth and this is not yet heaven, but what I can tell you is I have peace, joy, stability and see my life going from Glory to glory because now I know my gifts and my will is aligned with GOD's.

I may not know who you are, but I know God does, and He is very intentional, I believe that if you are reading this, then this is absolutely for you.

What are your gifts?

Is it writing, speaking, dancing, baking or are you a natural born leader maybe you are a leader who would rather give somebody else the spotlight but could be the backbone of a business or ministry. What did God put in your forming stages that you thought was a curse but is truly a blessing?

Before I became co-pastor, I was the leader of the "greeters" for a different congregation. One <u>Sunday morning</u> as we were gathering for prayer and preparation, one of the greeters in my team had an anxiety attack. I decided to separate her from the group and try my best to coach her through it since I am too familiar with those kinds of attacks. I told her "God is going to use you" that's when she stopped me and said "I'm so tired of everybody telling me that! Everybody tells me that, it's too cliché!" I could not agree with her more but here is the thing, it's the truth!

Let me explain, I usually use a "car repair tool kit" as an analogy, but because this book is dedicated to God's precious daughters, I'm going to write this analogy to be as relatable as possible. So, let's use a "make-up kit" (sorry men, you'll get in on the action in the next book) not that makeup is mandatory, but it just may be easier to understand, at least for me it is.

So, let's say you have an important gala to attend, but in your makeup kit you only have blush, can you really accomplish a full makeup look with just blush ? Or you only have eyeshadow, can you use that as face powder?

Please don't even try! No, you can't or at least you really, really shouldn't. You need different beauty tools for all the different areas of your face, eyes, eyebrows, lips, cheeks, etc... you need more than one tool! In the same way, God needs more than just one person to accomplish His greater plan, He has called us all because He needs us ALL!

We are the body of Christ; we are His beautiful bride. What part of the body are you? I know that a lot of powerful phrases have lost their value due to repetition, but it doesn't take away from the fact that they are true. God needs you! Yes, He can do anything because He is God, but He will not go against His own word and when the bible says we are co-participants of His divine nature, then that is what we are to be, participants.

Through these he has given us his very great and precious promises, so that trough them you may participate in the divine nature, having escaped the corruption in the world caused by evil desires.

2 Peter 1:4(NIV)

PARTICIPATE means WE need to WORK with GOD. I am part of the mouthpiece and my gift is that of a speaker, hence, me itching to talk whenever I can. Some of you are the ears because you have great listening gifts, others the feet because you are not afraid to move when He tells you to move, or maybe you are His eyes and can see through the eyes of mercy what many don't.

These are just examples to name a few, but there are so many more gifts.

Which do you have?

Who are you in the body of Christ?

How can He use what He so preciously created for the greater good of His beautiful kingdom?

You are so valuable and very much needed, but because you have been lied to for so long, you somehow stopped believing you are important and made for a higher purpose.

Why does the enemy of our souls hate us so much?

Why has he been trying to keep the truth hidden from us?

He is jealous of us, that's why!

God's love for us is so great, and He has given us so much authority that the enemy knows that if we know the truth, we will defeat him and advance God's kingdom faster. Here is an example that comes to mind that I believe hits the nail on the head when it comes to Satan and us. I want you to imagine that you had a boyfriend who is handsome, kind and an all-around "great catch". This boyfriend was so good to you, but you went for the 80/20, which means you left him for a good-looking guy that ended up treating you terribly and years later, you want your ex back. The only problem is, he is engaged to a beautiful woman, you see the way he sees her and loves her, and you know deep in your heart she is the love of his life, and she appreciates, loves and values him right back.

Would you be happy for her or feel a sense of bitterness, jealousy or even hate?

Satan is that ex that decided to go for the 80/20 he left everything for the possibility of having even more, more power, more privileges, more glory. Satan lost it all because he was too foolish to see that greatness of who God is and accept that only HE is GOD a triune GOD, Father, Son, and Holy Spirit. We are the beautiful bride that Jesus loves so much, the bride He DIED for, and we are the love of His life. Of course, the devil hates us; it's only normal. We took what he thinks is his, and now he wants to steal our peace, kill the promise before it comes to pass then ultimately destroy us.

The thief comes only to steal and kill and destroy; I have come that they may have life, and have it to the full.

John 10:10 (NIV)

If this sounds scary, I assure you it's really not. As a husband would do anything to protect his wife, so too will our Father in heaven move mountains on our behalf, not only that, He has given us the authority to move them ourselves. He has promised that even if the enemy tries to use things against us, God H imself will turn it around for our good, give us double for our trouble and trade our ashes for beauty.

Instead of your shame you will receive a double portion, and instead of disgrace you will rejoice in your inheritance. And so you will inherit a double potion in your land, and everlasting joy will be yours.

Isaiah 61:7(NIV)

If after you have done your part and aligned yourself with His Will, became clear about the Way in which He formed you, and the only thing now that is frustrating you is His TIME maybe this example can help. I don't want to take credit for it; I heard a preacher use this once. I want to paint the picture here, let's say you are wealthy and money is no issue for you, you have a son and your son wants a beautiful brand-new Ferrari. He dreams about this car every night. He can't stop talking about it; it's like he's obsessed! He wants that car, and he wants it NOW, but he is only 7 years old. Would you buy it for him and let him drive it? No, you wouldn't and not because you hate your son but because you love him so much that you know if he drove it instead of blessing him, you would be hurting him.

That for me was the hardest part to accept, that His Time is not my time, His Way, so not my way and that I needed to align myself with His Will because everything according to His Will is far better than my will could ever be. He's God I'm not, He knows I don't and honestly surrendering to that alone has blessed me with so much peace I never thought was possible. It took me quite some time to comprehend that God makes us wait for different reasons sometimes, He wants to work on us, sometimes, He wants to work on others and sometimes, He wants us to be so fulfilled in Him that when He decides to give us what we long for, it won't take us away from His Love. When we are willing to do His Will, in His Way and in His Time, we will maintain our focus on the Giver and not the gifts.

Chapter 4

Living Water

"This is it; this is where my life changes, all my troubles will go away because I will look BEAUTIFUL!!!" I said to myself as I began my pursuit of looking my absolute best. With a personal trainer, an expensive diet plan, a new wardrobe, contacts and some hair extensions, I was ready to take over the world. My view of myself was dependent on how Society viewed me, after all, we are "supposed" to look a certain way to be treated nicer and hold a higher value, right? After about three months when the results started kicking in, I felt great but only for a bit, I still felt lonely, and it seemed now that I could only go so far. There would always be something to fix on the outside that never took care of the problem on the inside.

Now it was time for a man! "Yes, that for sure will take my loneliness away and make me feel loved". I deceived myself once more and began the search for the "love of my life" Within a month of going anywhere I could to meet other men my age; I finally met "the one". He was tall, dark and handsome, we hit it off right away both feeling like it was "love at first sight," and within four months of our first date, we were engaged to be married. He was an Army Soldier and was ordered to move to Washington State where he would be stationed till further notice. I of course as any soon to be bride followed my future husband. I left California in pursuit of my "Happily ever after".

After only a few months I knew I had made a huge mistake, I was in a relationship only to fill an empty void and realized that we were just not compatible. I began feeling even more depressed than before and that hole in my heart, felt like it was only getting deeper. I needed a new pursuit, I began reaching out for the "American dream" I wanted to have more money, somehow, I convinced myself that more money meant more happiness and peace of mind. I was soon able to reach my goal of obtaining that money and lived an extravagant life of shopping for fun. It only took some time before the excitement of what I bought wore off, and that emptiness that I kept trying to eradicate peeked its ugly little face again. I remember an interview with a very famous Hollywood Star where she said "There is nothing worse than having it all and still feeling depressed" I was nowhere near having it all, but I was in a place where I had more than I ever did, and in that moment, I understood exactly what she meant. The "hot body," the handsome man and the money only served as confirmation that there is something in the human soul that can't ever be fulfilled by any source other than God.

Not wanting to relinquish all my life to Him just yet, I opted to explore what I was feeling and fix it myself. I would go to any doctor that would listen and try my best to convince them to give me a diagnosis and prescribe me pills that would relieve my pain. Even my best friend at the time "Alcohol" could not quench the thirst deep in my soul. It would numb it only for a bit, but it would come back with a vengeance that included anxiety attacks, and hangovers that felt more like near-death experiences.

Do not gaze at wine when it is red, when it sparkles in the cup, when it goes down smoothly! In the end it bites like a snake and poisons like a viper

Proverbs 23:31-32(NIV)

I was done looking for an external answer to an internal problem, when I finally for the first time in my life, asked the right question.

What could quench this thirst that not men, money, beauty, or even alcohol could? If not what, then who?

"but whoever drinks the water I give them will never thirst. Indeed, the water I give them will become in them a spring of water welling up to eternal life."

John 4:14(NIV)

I found my answer within the beautiful red letters in the Bible, "The living water" that's who, our Lord and Savior, Jesus Christ.

The creator of the universe also created you, He created you so that you can have communion with Him, and nothing else could ever satisfy that human need because it was not intended to be satisfied, any other way. The further from God you are, the emptier you will feel. He is the reason why we have breath in our lungs and were born into this world in the first place; it's His breath we breathe. The other day while I was preaching, God gave me a picture in my mind of the iPhone, as soon as I could, I put into words what I was receiving in my Spirit and was able to integrate it immediately into the sermon, and the Analogy I used went something like this.

When it comes to your cell phone, what does it take to keep it "On" aside from the button? It must be charged right? The device was created to need a source of energy to stay on and the more energy it has, the better it works. Let's pretend your cell phone has a mind of its own, and honestly sometimes I think it does. Now your phone refuses to get plugged in and instead, it tries to charge itself by other means, you and I both know that other than the charger and a source of energy (not counting in an extra battery of course, which would only suffice a little longer) this phone could not accomplish its goal. In the same way, if we are not "Plugged in" we too will die, maybe not physically but Spiritually and that type of death is far worse.

"I am the vine; you are the branches. If you remain in me and I in you, you will bear much fruit; apart from me you can do nothing.

John15:5(NIV)

As a woman who loves to have evidence of something happening IMMEDIATELY, this for me was the hardest part. The getting "Plugged in part". I wondered how I could have communion with a God that I could not see, feel, or hear. If I could compare it to something, it would be as if somebody asked me to "write Santa a letter" at 34 years old! It sounded Silly and at first, and it felt even sillier. Just like with the cell phone example, we don't see the energy being transferred into the phone, as humans, we don't see what God transfers in us when we choose to honor Him with our time in the Secret Place we use to pray. What felt silly at first, became the best choice of my life, a choice that allowed me to experience firsthand the supernatural power of God.

We think waking in Communion with God should be hard because after all, He's the Creator of the UNIVERSE!! The truth is, it's not! It's abnormally easy. God made walking with Him so easy that you might at first think you are doing it wrong. Before I begin to give you the meat of how to do it in practical terms, I really want you to understand the mind of God and these next Bible verses will help with that. I pray you get Spiritual Revelation of our Father's heart, If you can grasp this concept I promise you, it will change your life just like it did mine.

"Which of you fathers, if your son asks for a fish, will give him a snake instead? Or if he asks for an egg, will give him a scorpion? If you then, though you are evil, know how to give good gifts to your children, how

much more will your Father in heaven give Holy Spirit to those who ask him!"

Luke 11:11-13(NIV)

One God and Father of all, who is over all and through all and in all.

Ephesians 4:6 (NIV)

As a father has compassion on his children, so the LORD has compassion on those who fear him;

Psalm 103:13 (NIV)

I know in the past because of different manipulating and distorted reasons, that I really do not want to get too deep into, you probably believed that God was scary, mean and sends people to hell for Sport, right? Wrong, as a matter of fact, it is the Polar Opposite. The truth about our Father's heart is that He is loving, graceful, merciful and kind, HE LOVES YOU, not conditionally as the world loves but with love we can't even fathom. Your sadness makes Him sad, your sorrow breaks His heart and your belief system when not aligned with His, grieves Him deeply. All He can do is watch as we self-destroy what He so lovingly created until we ask Him to intervene and surrender all of our "rights".

Since the Bible uses an earthly father's heart in so many verses, let's use some examples we can relate to. I'm sure there are some truths I've shared that in your mind still don't add up. Those of you with adult children will find this first example easy to connect to. If your adult child was 25 years old and decided to go out drinking, experimenting with drugs and live their life in complete destruction, how would you feel? If he or she decided to move far out of your reach could you help them? What if your child decided to ask you for help, moved back home to be near you and was obedient to all the treatment that he or she needed, would you help your adult child then?

Here is another question I often get, I just got this question yesterday again by my 11-year-old daughter "If God is so loving then why does He send humans to hell?" Great question and again there is a simple answer, He doesn't, He gives us a choice, and we get to decide where we want to go.

For this example, I will speak to those of you who have teenage children that by law can decide who they want to live with. Let's pretend you are a considerably strict mother setting your child up for success. You encourage them to eat healthily, teach them the importance of responsibility and have them sleep early so they can be well rested for the next day.

Now "Rockstar life dad" gives them donuts for breakfast, allows them to make their own curfew, and lets them run free to do everything they wish, even if it's detrimental to their bodies. Do to this "night and day" type of upbringing your child decides to go with dad. Then how would you feel? Would you love them any less? Would your heart break? Does this mean you wanted to send them with dad? No, as heartbroken as you would be, you would let them make their choice and not love them any less.

This day I call the heavens and the earth as witnesses against you that I have set before you life and death, blessings and curses. Now choose life, so that you and your children may live and that you may love the LORD your God, listen to his voice, and hold fast to him. For the LORD is your life, and he will give you many years in the land he swore to give to your fathers, Abraham, Isaac and Jacob.

Deuteronomy 30:19-20 (NIV)

I will be the first one to admit that sin can be fun, at first, until it becomes an oppression that only God can free us from. So many people believe that God is somehow a mean God, who is in the business of taking all our fun away, we think Christianity is a "weird religion," and I don't even blame them. Some of those including myself have missed the mark in resembling who Christ is and what He stood for, LOVE. In our misconception, we confused a relationship with God with legalistic, religious traditions that tend to repel people instead of attracting them.

Yes, God tells us to live a certain way but not for His good, He does that for us! For OUR GOOD. Let's go back to the earlier example of the child who chose to go with the "Rockstar life dad" and the "strict boring mom" why did the mom set all of these rules for her child? Is it because she enjoys watching their child suffer without their morning donut? No, it's because she knows what's good and bad for her child. She loves her child too much to let her child auto destroy for the sake of instant gratification.

God loves you, and like any good father, He wants the best for you. He wants you healed and happy, news flash! God has been God for time immemorial, only ETERNITY. He knows what is best for us and what is not, what we were created for and the path we should take, He not only has wisdom, He created it! We can TRUST HIM! As much as I wish I could see Him with my physical eyes, speak to Him, hear Him audibly all the time, I can't, but not because He's not there. His kingdom is within us, and among us, you need only to build your faith through the power of His Word.

Once, on being asked by the Pharisees when the kingdom of God would come, Jesus replied, "The coming of the kingdom of God is not something that can be observed, nor will people say, 'Here it is' or 'There it is' , because the kingdom of God is in your midst."

Luke17:20:21(NIV)

Our wonderful loving father left us His Will, written in The Holy Bible. In it is written everything we should know to live prosperous and successful lives. It is the next best thing to God physically being with us and instructing us himself which paths to take. It is so specific and carries so much power that it will change your life in ways you can only dream of.

I'm sure you have heard of a "will" or "testament" if not I'll give you a brief explanation. Before a person dies, he or she can choose to leave instructions on who they want their property to go to. The person must be very specific because the "will" is a legal document that carries enough power as if the deceased was himself giving that person the property but since it only comes into effect the moment the person is physically gone that legal document would be considered the next best thing.

What would happen if a wealthy person wrote a "will" where he gives his son all his wealth, but the son never actually reads it? If the son just kept that document in his drawer to collect dust and never read it, would the son be able to collect all that wealth not knowing it was available to him?

That is exactly what happens to a lot of God's children who don't even realize all the wisdom, knowledge, revelation, and power that was written for them. I can tell you from personal experience that the Word of God, which is The Holy Bible, has all that we need to live a life worth living. It has our Father's Good Will written in it and power to create lasting transformation.

Keep this Book of the law always on your lips; meditate on it day and night, so that you may be careful to do everything written in it. Then you will be prosperous and successful.

Joshua1:8(NIV)

Let's now deal with my favorite topic; "communion with God" the definition of communion is "the sharing or exchanging of intimate thoughts and feelings, especially when the exchange is on a mental or spiritual level". This is why we were created in the first place, to have communion with Him. I remember hearing a sermon one day, where the preacher said she had been praying to go deeper with God but didn't know how. For a long time, she would pray, and there would be no real change no "Breakthrough" until she read a book written by Jeanne Guyon, that forever changed her life.

I decided to read the book myself and guess what? That same book changed my life also. The book is titled "Experiencing the depths of Jesus Christ," and it was published in 1685. In this book, Jeanne teaches about experiencing Christ in such a way that seemed too simple at first, but by the time I was done reading the book I realized, it was deep.

Ever since I could remember I had struggled when it came to prayer, it was just too hard and sometimes to be very honest, flat out boring. I went ahead and read this book, and it clicked! GOD is so easily accessible. He is always there with us and in us waiting on us to get Him out of our box and off our own agenda. We must be comfortable with the fact that we will NEVER, EVER fathom who God truly is and the magnitude of His power. Humbly come to Him without expecting an experience but just honoring Him with our time our Love and our undivided attention. He is worthy of it ALL!

I genuinely believe an ant has a better chance at learning how to use the Internet, than we do at understanding who God truly is and the might of His power, so we might as well stop and just fully surrender to Him in mind body and spirit. God is not intended to be complicated because He is not supposed to be understood, as a matter of fact, the less we rely on our understanding and just believe everything He says, the better our lives will be.

Trust in the LORD with all your heart and lean not on your own understanding; in all your ways submit to him, and he will make your paths straight.

Proverbs 3:5-6(NIV)

In our pursuit of Naturally understanding a Supernatural God, we have built so many rituals that He didn't even come up with in the first place. The rituals are more so for us than they are for Him. God wants us to trust Him, look to Him, spend time with Him, so He can align our spirit with His and Love us while we Love Him. When we no longer try to figure things out, then we enter into His resting place and find out just how light His burden really is.

"Come to me, all you who are weary and burdened, and I will give you rest. Take my yoke upon you and learn from me, for I am gentle and humble in heart, and you will find rest for your souls. For my yoke is easy and my burden is light."

Matthew 11:28-30(NIV)

Chapter 5

The biggest Misconception

What's wrong with your face? My mother asked as I tried my best to explain I got my "fanny" kicked by a girl much smaller than I. "I let Belen beat me up" I said "what? Why?" She asked with a confused look on her face. I could not find any other words that would make the decision I had just made sound sane, so, I went ahead and just said the truth "I had just confessed my sins to the priest mom, and God said we are to turn the other cheek, so I did, I just let her beat me up". I could tell that she had other words in mind to say, but she didn't, she said nothing else.

I attended a private school for 3 years to be exact, that made hell very real, and God seems very stern. I remember thinking to myself "that statue doesn't look very mean, so why is he so strict?" I would wonder if at night the statue left its place to go around the world looking for "good people" and "bad people" so he can send those doing bad things to hell on a "slipping slide". I was so terrified and don't get me wrong. The fear of the Lord is very important, but the root is far more important to where the fear comes from.

My perception as a child was so disconnected from the reality of the great "I AM" I serve today. I know now at thirty-four years old, that the fear of God I have is only due to the immense Love I feel for Him. When everybody had given up on me including my mother, He never did. I realized in a homeless shelter when I lost the support of friends and family that He is all I have and all I will truly ever need. The God that both you and I serve is so gracious, kind, loving and beyond powerful that I made a commitment in that shelter, to only live for Him from that moment on, it was no longer because I was afraid to go to hell but because I wanted to make my Father proud.

I find it so interesting how we want to experience only the "Good times" that bring us joy and laughter without realizing that it's those moments we dread, those moments of utter excruciating pain that can truly leave a lasting impact in our lives. It's moments of heartbreak when our ego is out the door that if we turn to God, He can use as a metamorphosis that will lead us towards a better path. It's that re-route where God becomes more than religion and legalism; He becomes pure unconditional Love.

I have experienced two "Rock Bottoms", one rock bottom I thought I got out of on my own and instead of becoming better I became bitter. The second rock bottom is where God called me into His marvelous light, and I was so tired of being tired, that I finally said YES. This second rock bottom was the best experience I have ever gone through, not because it felt good or anything like that, He alone knows how much my beautiful daughter and I suffered, but because it was in that season, I encountered His mercy like never before.

When others saw the failure, He saw the promise. I understood during those moments of brokenness that His desire was not to send me to hell but to love me into heaven. As lonely and afraid as I felt at different times, I knew deep in my spirit somehow, someway, He would turn all that mess into a powerful message, and He absolutely has. The God I was introduced to as a child and the God I know today could not be further apart.

It's as if when He called me in that dream to serve Him, the first thing He wanted to be striped away from me was the belief that God is like a kid with a magnifying glass burning ants enjoying their pain. He was very intentional in demonstrating that He is far above religious views and debates about the "small stuff". The God I misunderstood for so long reminded me every day that He loves me enough to have sent His only son to die on that cross to save me, a God that is the truest form of LOVE because God is LOVE!

Whoever does not love does not know God, because God is love.

1 John 4:8(NIV)

Pursuing a relationship with God has been the most exciting, peaceful, loving and rewarding experience of my life. This process has been as easy as going to dinner with a loved one, it has required some self-discipline because spiritual laziness is very real, but once it became a habit, it felt like second nature. I can honestly say that now I have the desire to sit in His presence in the morning, as soon as I wake up and at night right before I go to sleep. It's also quite normal to feel a bit silly at first because we are used to having a relationship with those we see, feel, hear and touch. Having a relationship with God requires us to go deeper than our human senses. One of the benefits of spending time with God is that it strengthens our Spiritual muscles and allows us to dive in, head first, into the realm of the unknown. That "Strange world" that many intellectuals perceive as nonsense, unreal or even ridiculous, however, I assure you, it is much more real than anything we have ever experienced before.

If you are afraid of what people will say, then I feel forced to warn you, you might have a harder time. Following God is not for the weak at heart. It's for the bold in Spirit who care more about what God says, than what the world says about them. This pursuit requires us to humble ourselves before the one and only true God and become as little children allowing Him the painful process of softening our callused heart created by years of pain and suffering. We must choose to be vulnerable and raw, so nothing could separate us from the experience of being under the shadow of the almighty in our most transparent and authentic state.

Jesus said, "Let the little children come to me, and do not hinder them, for the kingdom of heaven belongs to such as these."

Matthew 19:14(NIV)

But God chose the foolish things of the world to shame the wise; God chose the weak things of the world to shame the strong.

1 Corinthians 1:27(NIV)

The "Game changer" for me was written in the book "Experiencing the depths of Jesus Christ" which I mentioned in chapter four. Before I read that book, I felt as if my words were somehow not quite making it to heaven and I was only speaking to myself. I wanted to learn how to pray but did not have a clue how, since the way other people prayed just did not quite work for me. I began to read the book and found out why I was getting it all wrong; I learned that I should not create an agenda for myself or God that dictated what I ought to feel and by what time I should feel it. The only goal I should have set in mind is the goal to set apart some time for God and honor my relationship to Him like I would any human relationship that I wanted to pursue. I learned in that beautiful book to just position myself to receive whatever He wanted to give me in His time and not mine, my prayers became all about letting go and letting God.

I later found out this type of prayer is called "LISTENING prayer". The first time I tried what this book said to do, I struggled. I found it difficult just to be still and not think a million random thoughts, but the more I practiced, the more I said to myself "there is just no way communion with God is this easy", I would never have imagined that a 15 min listening prayer at the beginning, would lead to what is now my lifestyle. The way I hear from God today is so real that it has become a new normal from which all my decisions are made. I know this is only the beginning of my journey, but I can honestly say, I have never felt closer to the Father than I do right now. I have come to the realization that God is my vacation, not my duty; He is my restoration in moments of desperation.

By now you probably figured out that I love using examples to simplify a deeper revelation so here is another one. Let's say that you and your husband are out on "date night," and through the night he keeps falling asleep, looking at his watch, and is obvious about the fact that hanging out with you is more of a chore. You see a couple next to you and observe as the husband looks so present in that moment, enjoying his time with her and having fun.

Who would you think is a happier wife?

She of course, in that same way we must give God our best because believe it or not He has feelings, you know how I know? Because the bible tells us so.

And do not grieve the Holy Spirit of God, with whom you were sealed for the day of redemption.

Ephesians 4:30(NIV)

How could you grieve someone who doesn't have feelings? You can't. If we want quality time, then so does God. He wants you to enjoy getting to know Him, and the coolest thing of all is that He wants to show you, who He is, even more than you could ever want to get to know Him.

'Call to me and I will answer you and tell you great and unsearchable things you do not know.'

Jeremiah 33:3(NIV)

We need just to ask that He would give us ears to hear and eyes to see. Yes, God wants to reveal Himself to you in the purest form. He doesn't want you to think He is inaccessible, He wants to have communion with you. We were made for that; we were made to worship, love, and walk with God. He yearns for us to seek His face and go after His heart. It grieves Him to see His children suffer and know that they are only a choice away from happiness that surpasses all understanding, even in the midst of life's storms. The abundant life He promised is truly only one choice away. I don't know about you, but I want Him to look no further.

I want to become that worshiper in truth and in spirit that He desires, I want with all my heart to bring him great joy. DO YOU?

Yet a time is coming and has now come when the true worshipers will worship the Father in Spirit and in truth, for they are the kind of worshippers the Father seeks.

John 4:23(NIV)

Worshipers in TRUTH AND IN SPIRIT?! This means that there must be worshipers in lies and in the flesh. This made a lot of sense as to why the "church" has done more harm than good at times by pushing many people away with its legalistic and judgmental approach. If like many people, you have been grieved by Congregations, I would like to stand in the gap between you and them and apologize because sometimes congregations get it wrong. The more I read the bible and zoom in on the teachings of our Prince of Peace Jesus Christ the more I understand why we all have, at one point or another "missed the mark". Every time Jesus Rebuked someone, I noticed the party receiving the rebuking were religious leaders, not the "sinners". He could see through people's facade straight into their heart, Jesus was all about the heart!

But the LORD said to Samuel, "Do not consider his appearance or his height, for I have rejected him. The LORD does not look at the things people look at. People look at the outward appearance, but the LORD looks at the heart."

Samuel 16:7(NIV)

Now I am in no way saying that God is perfectly fine with us living comfortably with deliberate sin. The definition of Grace is an undeserved favor. This undeserved favor that God so generously gives does not serve as a pass to live in sin, it does, however, empower us to live above sin and do it from a place of Loving God so much, that we refuse to grieve Him on purpose. On the other hand, if we consider ourselves believers of Christ but refuse to put LOVE first, then we are only fooling ourselves and grieving God more than if we were just ignorant about His word. I can honestly tell you that this is what I believe grieves God the most. His own so-called people, judging, condemning and hating others, pretending to be something they are not. God is calling us to do it right! To walk the walk as His love ambassadors and anything that does not represent that is more detrimental than not serving God at all.

"Beware of these teachers of religious law! For they like to parade around in flowing robes and love to receive respectful greetings as they walk in the marketplaces. And how they love the seats of honor in the synagogues and the head table at banquets. Yet they shamelessly cheat widows out of their property and then pretend to be pious by making long prayers in public. Because of this, they will be severely punished."

Luke 20:46-47(NLT)

One day as I was reading the book of Revelation it hit me! WE need to get it together and stop pretending that we got this in the bag. The truth is, we are weak without God, and without him we truly don't stand a chance. The book of Revelations touched on something that was ALARMING, to say the least.

It's important that I mention this because most people think that all Congregations are good representatives of Jesus and they are not. I really hate to say this, but the truth is, most congregations are not living as God commands, it's BIBLICAL. In a Nutshell, the book of Revelations talks about the 7 churches and how 5 of those get it wrong. Here is the list so you can see for yourself what God commands the churches to do to get back in alignment with His will.

(I am not writing the following verbatim, but you can find it in Revelation 2:1-29 and it continues unto Revelation 3:1-22 for your own research which I highly recommend)

1) EPHESUS; Rekindle your desire for your first Love

2) Smyrna; Overcome your fear stay faithful

3) Pergamum: Guard your heart against false teaching

4) Thyatira; Don't tolerate false teaching or immorality

5) Sardis; Strengthen what remains and wake up

6) Philadelphia; Hold fast to your faith persevere

7) Laodicea; Zealously repent and don't be lukewarm

These churches are a representation of all the people following Christ, and as humans we are flawed. Therefore, we must become rooted in His word and constantly learn to listen to what His next step for our individual journey is. The only way to achieve this ability to hear Him is by maintaining a close relationship with God. WE NEED to wake up to the truth of what He expects us to be. Transparent, humble, and self-aware of our human limitations.

I too walked away from the "Church", several years ago and now that I am back, I can see clearly the difference between relationship and religion. If you walked away from God because people did not represent Him right, I hope this knowledge of the seven churches in the book of "Revelation" helps you understand that what you did not approve of, God does not approve of either but here is the "thing", judgment belongs to the Lord and not us.

God gave me a vision one day that I believe He wants me to share in this book. I saw a hospital and a lot of sick people and God asked me deep in my spirit, "Would you still see that doctor if there were this many people waiting for him at the lobby" I said, "yes Lord, the doctor must be really good if all these people are here to see him". Then the Lord said to me "I am the GREAT PHYSICIAN, do not judge those that come to see me for they are seeking healing for their souls" It made so much sense, I now only focus on the Lord and let Him do the judging.

When Jesus heard this, he told them, "Healthy people don't need a doctor-sick people do. I have come to call not those who think they are righteous, but those who know they are sinners."

Mark 2:17(NLT)

May we walk in Love and forgiveness to be true representatives of God, who is one with Jesus.

Don't you believe that I am in the Father, and that the Father is in me? The words I say to you I do not speak on my own authority. Rather, it is the Father, living in me, who is doing his work.

John 14:10 (NIV)

Let's make peace with what was and return to Christ to become the church that gets it right. If in this very moment you are thinking "No, I can't do this, too much damage was done, and God could never understand" Let me remind you that Jesus was human too, and He underwent suffering that most of us can't even comprehend, He understands you. He knows what it's like to be heartbroken, rejected, abused, and betrayed. He wants to be involved in your healing journey and in literally every area of your life. Whether you struggle with emptiness, loneliness, self-doubt, shame or all of the above. He wants to turn it all around for your good. God is the only one that turns messes into messages and tests into testimonies. With His Grace, mercy, and love He wants to bring you into His resting place. A place where everything that the devil used to try to destroy you, will now be used by God to anoint you. I may not know you, but GOD does, and He LOVES you, He yearns for you, and He has amazing plans for your life!

'For I know the plans I have for you," declares the LORD, "plans to prosper you and not to harm you, plans to give you hope and a future."

Jeremiah 29:11(NIV)

"Experiencing the depths of Jesus Christ"

Synopsis

https://www.lizfuerteministries.com/p/ thank-you-EXPERIENCING-THE-DEPTHS-OF-JESUS-CHRIST-Synopsis

Chapter 6

More precious than Rubies

Are you ready to be a mom? A lady whom I had never seen before but felt familiar to, said to me, "No I am so not ready" I replied, "you will be a mom in the next month" she said to me, and immediately I woke up. "Thank you, Jesus; It was only a dream," I thought to myself not realizing I would find out some weeks later that in fact, I was pregnant. I remember hearing my daughter's name for the first time at a shopping mall near my house, "Amaris come here" a mother said to her beautiful little girl, "Excuse me, ma'am, what is her name?" I asked her. I had never heard that name before, but it was as if that was the perfect name for my baby, who I was certain would be a girl. As soon as I got home that day, I turned on my computer and searched the web to see, what that name meant. "GIFT FROM GOD" "that's it," I thought to myself "that's her name!! Hello Amaris, now I can speak to you by your name."

As she grew up, I remember moments where I would just stare at her thinking "she is so perfect; I love her eyes, her nose, her smile, her lashes, she is just PERFECT". Even when I would speak about my dear Amaris, I could not help but show the love I have in my heart for her through the window of my watering eyes. I felt love, I never knew was even possible, no matter how mad or frustrated I would get with her, no matter how many mistakes a day she'd make, she was still the apple of my eye and my love for her was never any less. I had never experienced this kind of love before. The love of a mother.

As I began to read the bible and learn about the everlasting love of God, I could not help but to imagine, what it must feel like to love people so much and see them believe the lies in their head about what they are not. As a mother to a beautiful young lady, I have this soft side for women, and when I speak publicly at events that are targeted towards women, I always pray for God to allow me to see them the way He sees them, and He absolutely does. I see all these beautiful little girls who just wanted to be loved, and because of different traumatic events, they are now left picking up the pieces of their shattered heart. I see the light in their eyes clouded by desperation as they look to me for a word that would give them some peace if only for a moment. I could also sense our Father's heart breaking as He waits patiently with open arms for His beautiful daughters to just come home. His home where His Spirit dwells, in that secret place of your choosing. As I see them, I see my beautiful Amaris, and for a second I get to perceive how perfectly imperfect and beautifully broken they are, I see all the ashes that only God can turn into beauty.

YOU ARE BEAUTIFUL, SPECIAL, AND IMPORTANT TO GOD; YOU ARE THE APPLE OF HIS EYE!

I know that you might believe that your choices are your Identity, but that is just not so. Those are just that, choices, the truth about how God formed you as a Woman to be, is so incredibly beautiful, that it might be hard to digest but here is my attempt to simplify it.

Let's use cars for this analogy. When a company like Volkswagen makes a car like a Beetle, for example, it begins with just a blank sheet of paper and some rough sketches, after that, the car takes shape in the form of a clay model and then it's off to production by different robots who used the same pressing tools with the utmost precision to make sure all the cars have the same core. However, even though the core is the same, each car is unique with a specific Vehicle Identification number and of course then you have the colors and different things that make each car fit the type of person they are designed for, but the mold is the same. I know you are far more valuable than any car and you are way more unique than a Volkswagen Beetle, but the point I am trying to make is that God created all of His women to have the same core. He created us to be amazing women that succeed in every area of our lives because we were made to be more than conquerors.

Do you know that you are a GIFT from God to your husband or future husband, if like me yours is on his way?

The truth is, we have really no need to look for a husband because if he is from GOD then he will be doing all the heavy lifting and searching for us. We need only to fix our eyes on God and allow Him to do the healing and transformation that He needs to do in them and in us so that instead of a blessing to our husbands, we don't become their curse. The Bible is clear that when the right husbands find us, they will find favor from God. I mean HELLO do you not see your value yet? Girl, you are all that and a bag of Flaming Hot Cheetos!

He who finds a wife finds what is good and receives favor from the LORD.

Proverbs 18:22(NIV)

I speak to so many women who refuse to be alone and settle for anyone even if they are far from what God intended for them. I used to go from relationship to relationship that culminated in dead ends and broken hearts. All due to my inability to wait, anyone that knows me personally knows that I am very comfortable with being single now and waiting on God's plan for marriage in my life. It is much worse to be with the wrong person than it is to remain single; I know that for a fact. I see the need for help in this area, and at the end of this chapter, I will provide you with a link to an Article I wrote that might help if you struggle with being alone.

Along with being a gift, we are made to be hard workers, this ability was installed in us in the formation period, we have the anointing to attract prosperity. We have it in us to be resourceful, loving nurtures who raise our sons to be mighty men after God's own heart, and daughters to become mighty women who are the apple of God's eye. We not only think about today, we think about yesterday, tomorrow, the day after and years to come. When you need multitasking, leave it to the woman, men need not apply, why? Cause we were built that way. We are brave women that endure the most excruciating pain in the giving birth process. We get to partner up with God and give LIFE!

We have it in us to be wise in our finances and have such a natural connection to God that we are sensitive to those less fortunate than us. We are compassionate human beings that see the world much deeper than most men can. We have it in us to want to feel beautiful, and we can make it happen by choosing to wear nice things and by nice I don't mean expensive I mean beautiful in your perception.

We were made to support and help our husbands and children become what GOD has called them to be. We are all "BOSSES" ladies; I don't mean that from a place of arrogance but a place of capacity, whether you choose to stay home or join the corporate world, you are capable of great accomplishments. We are not intended to be a burden to anybody in any way. When we chose to live life the way God intended for us to live it, respect and admiration from our families will come with the territory.

Yes, ladies, that's in the bible! We were never meant to remain on the sidelines and blend in; we were made to stand out. WE have in us the ability to WALK THE WALK but please don't take my word for it, for it is WRITTEN

Who can find a virtuous and capable wife?
She is more precious than rubies.
Her husband can trust her,
and she will greatly enrich his life.
She brings him good, not harm,
all the days of her life.

She finds wool and flax
and busily spins it. She is like a merchant's ship,
bringing her food from afar.
She gets up before dawn to prepare breakfast for her household
and plan the day's work for her servant girls.

She goes to inspect a field and buys it;
with her *earnings she plants a vineyard.*
She is energetic and strong,
a hard worker.
She makes sure her dealings are profitable;
her lamp burns late into the night.

Her hands are busy spinning thread,
her fingers twisting fiber.
She extends a helping hand to the poor
and opens her arms to the needy.

She has no fear of winter for her household,
for everyone has warm clothes.

She makes her own bedspreads.
She dresses in fine linen and purple gowns.
Her husband is well known at the city gates,
where he sits with the other civic leaders.
She makes belted linen garments
and sashes to sell to the merchants.

She is clothed with strength and dignity,
and she laughs without fear of the future. When she
speaks, her words are wise,
and she gives instructions with kindness.
She carefully watches everything in her household
and suffers nothing from laziness.

Her children stand and bless her.
Her husband praises her:
"There are many virtuous and capable women in the
world,
but you surpass them all!"

Charm is deceptive, and beauty does not last;
but a woman who fears the LORD will be greatly
praised.
Reward her for all she has done.
Let her deeds publicly declare her praise.

Proverbs 31:10-31(NLT)

This is your MOLD!!! We may all have different looks, styles, personalities upbringing, etc. However, we have all of this installed in us.

We have believed the lies of the enemy who has used friends, family, strangers and our own mind to distort God's truth. I remember driving one day through skid row and asking God, why? Why is there so much suffering, addiction, homelessness and desperation in the world? I heard very clearly in my Spirit "My people die because of lack of knowledge."

My people are being destroyed because they don't know me. Since you priests refuse to know me, I refuse to recognize you as my priests. Since you have forgotten the laws of your God, I will forget to bless your children.

Hosea 4:6(NLT)

I want you to have this knowledge, so you can then choose from a place of wisdom and revelation, not desperation. This truth that comes straight from our Father's heart is what took me from homelessness, alcoholism, rage, and desperation to stability, peace, hope and LOVE! I want you to know who you truly are, so you can become everything you are called to be. I can never stress enough how much God wants to use you for His kingdom, how valuable you are to Him and how much He LOVES You. The person that is writing this book today is not the same person I was three years ago, and all the Glory belongs to

God for giving me the revelation of who I am and most importantly whose I am......HIS!

I understand the fact that not everyone has a desire to teach or preach the gospel because we all have different roles in the body of Christ; none is more valuable than the other. I do believe, however, we all have powerful stories that God wants to turn into testimonies and use to serve others. We have all experienced different heartbreaks and have seen God's Grace in different areas of our lives, where God can get all the Glory and serve another who is undergoing the same struggle. Not one person I have ever met has the same story, but every story I have ever heard can have great impact and direct a person towards the path of hope.

Still not convinced, here are some more verses that I pray will help you see the truth of who you really are and all that you can do.

No, in all these things we are more than conquerors through him who loved us.

Romans 8:37(NIV)

The LORD will make you the head, not the tail. If you pay attention to the commands of the LORD your God that I give you this day and carefully follow them, you will always be at the top, never at the bottom.

Deuteronomy 28:13(NIV)

I praise you because I am fearfully and wonderfully made; your works are wonderful, I know that full well.

Psalm 139:14 (NIV)

But you are a chosen people, a royal priesthood, a holy nation, God's special possession, that you may declare the praises of him who called you out of darkness into his wonderful light.

1 Peter 2:9(NIV)

YOU ARE FEARFULLY, AND WONDERFULLY MADE???

Too many times I hear women tell me that they don't feel important enough or qualified to help others, and that is a lie from the pit of hell. If you still have breath in your lungs, then there is still a mission you can choose to complete. If we stop comparing ourselves to each other and focus on our race, we won't feel so inadequate because there is nothing to compare the "inadequacy" to. God does not make mistakes, and He definitely does not make trash, insulting who you are is insulting who He is. You are His creation, His beautiful masterpiece and if you think you have gone through too many things for God to use you, then I invite you to reframe that because if anything, all that pain can only make you overqualified.

The other day as I was driving with my 11-year-old daughter I watched her look into the mirror and say to herself "My forehead is too big; my teeth are ugly" and at that moment I understood the heartbreak He must feel when we say all these negative things about what He so lovingly and carefully made. Even though I am only her mother, not her creator I could not help but feel sad and angry that she would say that about the forehead I love to kiss and those teeth that shine so bright every time she smiles. I then asked her "Amaris Compared to who"?

She gave me a perplexed look while I continued asking her "who are you comparing yourself to?" She said "No one" I just think it's too big. I told her what I'm about to tell you now. When you speak bad about you in that way, you are not just speaking about "You" you are in fact and without even intending to, speaking badly about the one who created you. When you speak words that instead of blessing you, curse you, then you are participating with the one who hates your Soul and confirming everything he wants you to see. Choose today to see yourselves through the eyes of God who made you exactly as you need to be.

When the voices of the enemy come, never repeat them out loud. Don't give those words life in your Spirit. It's of high importance for you to learn to discern, where your thoughts are coming from and speak the word of God against the ones that are coming from the enemy. We live in a broken world where society has normalized speaking to ourselves in an abusive manner as if we are our own possession, but the Bible is clear about the fact that we are not our own, we belong to God.

Do you not know that your bodies are temples of the Holy Spirit, who is in you, whom you have received from God? You are not your own;

1 Corinthians 6:19(NIV)

Speak life into yourself, speak life into your children, speak life into everything that surrounds you including your situations. I want to stress something very important in this chapter. Who God says you are and who Satan says you are must have a final vote to become a reality in your life. You get to choose whose voice you want to co-create with. The bible says that we are made in the image of God, and it also says that God spoke things into existence.

So God created man in his own image; in the image of God He created him; male and female He created them.

Genesis 1:27(NKJV)

This means that you create by what you speak. As rooted as I want you to be in the word of God, I understand that our humanity needs some type of proof, something to work with as we mature and grow in our faith. So here is scientific proof that can back up what is written in the Holy Bible.

There was a study done by Dr. Masaru Emoto who was a renowned scientist in Japan. Dr. Emoto did a research concerning "water memory" based on samples of frozen water, he managed to photograph crystals formed by water. And according to the quality, and the "messages" sent to the water; the presence and the quality of the crystals would turn out completely different. The more positive the words or music played near the water, the more beautiful each crystal became.

Dr. Emoto went ahead and conducted another ground-breaking experiment where he placed rice into three glass beakers and covered them with water. Every day for a month he said thank you to one beaker, you are an idiot to the second and the third one, he completely ignored. After one month the rice that had been thanked began to ferment giving off a strong pleasant aroma. The rice in the second beaker turned black, and the rice that was ignored began to rot. When Dr. Emoto was interviewed about this experiment, he said he felt that this experiment provides an important lesson for all of us.

The adult human body is composed of 70% water, which means, what we speak and hear affects us in ways science is just now exploring.

God knows all of these secrets because HE CREATED THEM. He knows that sweet words soothe the soul.

Pleasant words are like a honeycomb, Sweetness to the soul and health to the bones.

Proverbs 16:24(NKJV)

Guess who also knows these laws? The enemy of course, and we must remember that he has come to still, kill and destroy and he will use anything he can use, including our own words against others and ourselves. The enemy of our

81

souls has been plotting against us since we were children, so as an adult, I ask you to please speak to your inner child with love, compassion, and grace. Don't neglect yourself because you are important and speak words that are the truth. The TRUTH about who God says you are! MORE PRECIOUS THAN RUBIES!

"Being alone without feeling lonely"

Article

https://www.lizfuerteministries.com/p/
Thank-You-Being-alone-without-feeling-lonely-Offer

Chapter 7

You don't have to be ready you just have to be willing

"Everything ok?", I asked our Ministry leader as she was scanning through the Bible with an overwhelmed expression on her face. I knew she was familiar with the scripture because she has been a God-fearing woman for a long time, so I was puzzled as to why she was feeling that way. "Our Pastor is not coming in today, he woke up feeling sick, and we have nobody to cover for him which means I'll have to preach". I could tell she was feeling anxious, so I offered to help with the preparation part. I then said, "I know!! I can write down some questions on flashcards, and we can make this more of an interactive sermon".

" I have a better idea" she said "You give the message Liz". Immediately, the first thing that came to mind was the fact that I looked like I had just rolled out of bed and there was cheese all over my pants because my intention was to serve food that day, not preach the gospel in front of everyone!! I began to have tunnel vision and my mouth dried up while experiencing the fight or flight response. I imagined myself running out of there as fast as I could and right when I was about to say no, I remembered a dream I had earlier that same week and it played in my head like a movie on a big screen.

"I want you to go to the Nations, share your testimony and feed my people."

Even in my dream, I knew it was the voice of God that was preparing me for what was to come "Ok, I'll do it" I told my leader as I began to prepare. I remember right before service, looking up at the sky wondering why God did not give me enough time to prepare properly for my debut as a teacher of the gospel. I was also wondering how out of a little paragraph I could speak for an hour and not run out of things to say. Fear began to creep in as I closed my eyes and said "Lord, I know this is your will, I can see your hand all over it, and both you and I know I am NOT READY. I'm internally freaking out here, but I don't want to disappoint you, so wherever you tell me to go as long as it's clear that it's you, I will go. I do, however, want to make a request, please open up heaven and give me all the help that I need for what you have called me to do, you are God, and you are able!"

As I pushed through the fear, I could sense the peace of God and this boldness began to take over me. I wish I could be specific about that message, but I honestly don't remember much. All I could remember were the faces of those brought to tears by the message and realizing that I didn't even touch my notes. When the leaders held hands at the end of service for our weekly closing prayer, we all looked around because we thought someone was blasting the AC. As the wind blew through our hair and understanding that there was no outside source, we all just looked at each other and smiled. We knew the Spirit of God wanted to make His presence known.

Driving home, I remember being in awe of what God had done that morning, His timing, His presence; His faithfulness became that much more real. I understood why things had to happen the way they did. He gave me the dream because He knew that opportunity was coming since He brought it forth, He also knew how afraid I would be and allowed me to be unprepared, so I could see His power in my weakness and not give credit to my skill or preparation of the delivery of the sermon. He is the one that touched people's hearts; I like the analogy that one preacher used when he said, "We are the box, God is the pizza, the box itself is not worth much but without the box how would they deliver the pizza?" The power and the Glory belong to God, and I'm just glad He uses us when we say YES to partnering up with Him in delivering what is so rightfully His.

Now that I get to preach on a regular basis, I have become cognizant of the fact that I must follow the Holy Spirit's agenda and not the other way around. I have also learned that transparency and authenticity are key elements if we truly want to do the Father's will. The Bible is clear about the fact that God can't stand hypocrisy. I enjoy being vulnerable because I know it pleases him and promotes breakthrough in others. In saying this, I am going to let you in on a little secret to emotionally prepare you for what is to come. READY? It's not going to be easy, none of what I am writing in this book will be easy. Every day, every minute and every second you will get to choose between instant gratification and self-discipline.

The choices that will feel unnatural at first will be the best choices for your life; they will propel you towards your destiny and into the promised land God tailormade just for you. Your part is to seek His face, and He will do the rest, walk in obedience and pray for help in the areas that feel more like a chain than a choice, surrender your control and learn to trust in Him. So many times, I have heard people say that the reason why they don't follow God is that they fear the devil will come after them, and that's another trick the enemy uses to keep us away. The truth is, you are already at war without realizing it, the difference now is you are on the winning side. Opposition is inevitable, and the flesh which is your human nature is going to be tested like never before, but as the fruit of the Spirit ripens in you, it will become easier and easier to overcome any obstacle.

For the flesh lust against the Spirit, and the Spirit against the flesh; and these are contrary to one another, so that you do not do the things that you wish.

Galatians 5:17(NKJV)

Not letting the flesh win is going to be a process and you will require much patience. In the beginning, it will feel as if you are taking two steps forward and four steps back. Without developing some level of patience, it will be a lot easier to give up and give in to what feels like a failure. I am convinced that the way the enemy usually makes his greatest move is by tempting you first and then shaming you so that you give up on your walk with God altogether. I've used this example before while preaching and I feel that this would be a good time to use it again.

The enemy is very much like a bully at fat camp who knows your weakness for candy and taunts you all day with it. Once you go for the bait, he then tells you "You see, you are just weak, too screwed up to ever reach your goal", he does exactly that but uses things much more powerful than candy to rail you in. The way to overcome the enemy in this area is to just run towards God even in your sin. Every morning when the sun rises and every evening when it sets ask God to forgive you and fill you with His undeserving Grace. Ask Him for help in the areas you keep failing at, and as soon as you ask Him for help and forgiveness, He will pull you closer in and begin what only He can do. I'm not telling you to deliberately sin knowing that no matter what He will forgive you, what I am saying is that in the areas that you feel the weakest in, He can give you the most power.

There are many promises in your life along with challenges on the way, but if there is still breath in your lungs, then there is a mission for you to complete. God has already equipped you with everything you need to complete all

He has called you to do. We serve a God that loves us, and we can trust that He will never set us up for failure. Your desires have already been paired up with the talents required to make any dream a reality. Trust in God make your move and watch in awe as He provides the Super to your Natural the moment He tells you to GO!

There is a story in the bible about the apostle Peter; this story is a representation of what many of us go through when God calls us to do something we believe exceeds our capacity.

Shortly before dawn Jesus went out to them, walking on the lake. When the disciples saw him walking on the lake, they were terrified. "It's a ghost," they said, and cried out in fear. But Jesus immediately said to them: "Take courage! It is I. Don't be afraid." "LORD, if it's you," Peter replied, "tell me to come to you on the water." "Come," he said. Then Peter got down out of the boat, walked on the water and came toward Jesus. But when he saw the wind, he was afraid and, beginning to sink, cried out, "LORD, save me!" Immediately Jesus reached out his hand and caught him. "You of little faith," he said, "why did you doubt? "And when they climbed into the boat, the wind died down. Then those who were in the boat worshiped him, saying, "Truly you are the Son of God".

Mathew 14:25:33(NIV)

When I read this profound passage, I could not help but make a couple of different observations. When Peter saw Jesus walking on water, he didn't say "Wait Lord, I'm not ready let me go change into some swimwear or wait I need to get some floaties (I bet even then, they had some type of water wear and equipment). Notice, he was the one that asked Jesus "Tell me to come" Jesus didn't ask him to come until Peter requested to be asked.

How many times have you prayed "Lord Please bless me with a Job, or a house or a ministry" then when God gives you opportunities, you become afraid and back down? Thinking "no, that job would be way too hard", or "I can finally afford that house but what if I lose it"? Or even "I believe God is calling me into ministry, but I can't do it now, I'm too flawed, and I just don't feel ready. I'm going to wait for this that and the other, then when the time is right, I'll do it". I bet Peter wasn't "ready", yet, he got out of the boat and did something SUPERNATURAL as everyone else stayed in the comfort of the boat and watched Peter WALK ON WATER.

I love the quote "anything worth doing is worth doing poorly until you learn to do it well" I get the feeling that the reason why Jesus chose Peter as the "rock where He would build His church" is because He could trust Peter with taking action despite his shortcomings. Peter was not successful in his attempt to reach Jesus, and when he took his focus from the Prince of Peace onto the wind, he began to sink. Jesus so lovingly helped him float again, quieted the wind, and got him back on the boat. The Lord did not tell Peter "See that's what you get" or "die you heathen, that's what you deserve for not trusting me" NO, He said, "You of little faith, why did you doubt?" and kept Peter safely by His side.

The last observation in this passage that I want to share with you is that when the other disciples saw what Jesus did for Peter, they were in awe and worshiped Him and finally believed what Jesus had said all along. They initially thought Jesus was a ghost and I believe that had it not been for Peter walking on the water which required Jesus to save him personally, they probably would have woken up the next day still believing it was a ghost. It took for one of them to step out of the safety of the boat and take a step towards Jesus, for Jesus to take a step towards him and the result was that they all believed.

I wonder what would happen, if like Peter we all chose to step out of our comfort zone and trust God even if we don't succeed at first. I also wonder how many people would be saved by seeing the power of God working in our lives. When God told me to write this book in my Spirit, I was really afraid. I was not ready, and writing was not my "forte", or so I thought. I was hesitant and doubtful looking for ways to get out of writing this book. English is not even my first language! I can't even write an Email without mistakes in it, and when I send text and read them back to myself, they don't even make sense to me.

When I made the choice to get out of my comfort zone and push through the fear I said, "Alright let's do this" and immediately began plotting ways to bring this book into existence in the easiest way possible. I looked into speaking and then transcribing it, so I could get out of the dread of typing the book myself, but God was very clear on the way He wanted to bring this book about, I was to TYPE it out.

When I received a clear confirmation that this was His Will, I began to sob like a little girl whose mom told her to pick up her room. I did not want to do it!!! I cried and cried and then finally I said, "OK Lord I will walk in obedience and partner up with you in this project, I ask for your divine downloads so that I can just be the typist." I then wiped off my tears and began the journey. Three weeks later the book was done, God is so faithful to keep His part of the deal if we only say YES, He truly will take care of the rest.

There will also be times where what God asks you to do will require cooperation from other people. A "team" and it Is intended to be that way for different reasons. When He asks us to do something that we can do best cooperatively, then He will also provide the right people for us. He is so intentional and provides absolutely all that we need.

When the Lord spoke to Moses in the land of Egypt, he said to him, "I am the Lord! Tell Pharaoh, the king of Egypt, everything I am telling you." But

Moses argued with the Lord, saying, "I can't do it! I'm such a clumsy speaker! Why should Pharaoh listen to me? "Then the Lord said to Moses, "Pay close attention to this. I will make you seem like God to Pharaoh, and your brother, Aaron, will be your prophet. Tell Aaron everything I command you, and Aaron must command Pharaoh to let the people of Israel leave his country.

Exodus 6:28-30 and continues onto Exodus 7:1-2(NLT)

What is God telling you to do?

What have you been putting off because you don't feel ready or qualified to do?

You are important enough to advance His kingdom and inspire change for the better, not only for your own life but the lives of many! Please, I beg of you, push through the fear, push through the doubt and take a step of faith. The God that we serve who loves us will always do His part, and it only takes one move of God to leave everyone in AWE!

On the last and greatest day of the festival, Jesus stood and said in a loud voice, "Let anyone who is thirsty come to me and drink. Whoever believes in me, as Scripture has said, rivers of living water will flow from within them." By this he meant the Spirit, whom those who believed in him were later to receive. Up to that time the Spirit had not been given, since Jesus had not yet been glorified.

John 7:37-39(NIV)

Afterword

Thank you for reading this book. Many women suffer, but the few who choose to believe, survive. The book is about women who go through hard times, yes, this is real. That's why we need wisdom and strength. Let us pray, "Father God, please help us for without thee, we are nothing. Help us to see with the sight reserved for us, in your mighty name, Amen." Life brings us many challenges, but we can face them with the word of God.

Thank you for reading, God Bless.

Amaris Elizabeth Parra

FREE Bonus Gifts

"7 easy yet POWERFUL questions that are sure to give you clarity about your purpose"

Worksheet

https://www.lizfuerteministries.com/p/
free-gift-7-easy-yet-POWERFUL

"Experiencing the depths of Jesus Christ"

Synopsis

https://www.lizfuerteministries.com/p/
thank-you-EXPERIENCING-THE-DEPTHS-OF-
JESUS-CHRIST-Synopsis

"Being alone without feeling lonely"

Article

https://www.lizfuerteministries.com/p/
Thank-You-Being-alone-without-feeling-lonely-Offer

Bibliography

Scripture verses marked NIV are taken from the NEW INTERNATIONAL VERSION.

Scripture verses marked NLT are taken from the NEW LIVING TRANSLATION.

Scripture verses marked KJV are taken from the KING JAMES VERSION.

Scripture verses marked NKJV are taken from the NEW KING JAMES VERSION

Guyon, Jeanne "EXPERIENCING THE DEPTHS OF JESUS CHRIST" published in 1685.

About the Author

Elizabeth Nova Fuerte is the Co-Pastor of Motel Ministry and Founder of Liz Fuerte Ministries. Elizabeth became a superwoman for the kingdom of God after experiencing Domestic Violence, Alcoholism, and Homelessness which she now calls her "Rock bottom and breakthrough experience". She is a writer, entrepreneur, life coach and public speaker. Her life changed when she heard the audible voice of God call her from darkness into light.

She is now determined to bring as many souls with her to experience the greatest Love of all, the unconditional LOVE of GOD!

Made in the USA
Las Vegas, NV
18 November 2020

11053315R00065